CORPORATE

CORPORATE INSOLVENCY FOR GENERAL PRACTITIONERS

by

Michael Griffiths
LLB, LLM, ACIArb

Senior Lecturer in Law
University of Wolverhampton

CLT PROFESSIONAL PUBLISHING
A DIVISION OF CENTRAL LAW TRAINING LTD

Published by
CLT Professional Publishing
A Division of Central Law Training Ltd
Wrens Court
52-54 Victoria Road
Sutton Coldfield
Birmingham B72 1SX

ISBN 1 85811 057 2

DTP by Book Production Services

Printed in Great Britain by Ipswich Book Company

Contents

Preface

This is essentially a notebook for general practitioners outlining the salient points of corporate insolvency law. For reasons best known to themselves, neither the Law Society nor any major accounting body seems to put insolvency law very high on the list of priorities for final examination level and so there ·is a frequent likelihood that litigators, commercial conveyancers, auditors etc will have but a scant knowledge of the subject. There are, of course, many excellent specialist books on insolvency, but, I believe, relatively few which concentrate on general principles alone.

In writing this book, I have followed the principle of early Roman warfare - divide and conquer. It is designed as a notebook with numbered paragraphs and copious subheadings. Moreover, since it is an outline, I have completely avoided footnotes and kept caselaw references to a minimum. Later notebooks in this series will provde more detail on specific areas. In this first notebook I have tried to ensure that readers can distinguish the wood from the trees.

Whenever I write I think with gratitude of R H Evans, solicitor, now retired, who, more than anyone, taught me to think about what I was trying to write and express myself with clarity. It was also he who suggested I might write "Griffiths on Going Under", a title which did not find favour with the publishers. I also owe a considerable debt to all those solicitors and accountants who, attending seminars which I have given on this subject, have asked questions which have caused me to think of matters concerning insolvency law which otherwise would never have occurred to me. Finally, I must express my thanks to the publishers for their considerable encouragement and support throughout this project.

The errors and shortcomings which remain are, of course, my own.

Michael Griffiths
University of Wolverhampton
March 1996

Abbreviations

CA	Companies Act 1985
CDDA	Company Directors Disqualification Act 1986
IA	Insolvency Act 1986
IR	Insolvency Rules 1986 (as amended)
LPA	Law of Property Act 1925

Table of Cases

Table of Statutes

INSOLVENCY PRACTITIONERS

Insolvency Practitioners

1. At the heart of all insolvency work today is the insolvency practitioner.

2. Only a properly licensed person may act as an insolvency practitioner. Authorisation of an insolvency practitioner may come from a recognised professional body such as the Law Society or the Institute of Chartered Accountants of England and Wales or from the Secretary of State for Trade and Industry.

3. As well as having authorisation, an insolvency practitioner must have proper insurance cover. (IA s 390 (3))

4. An insolvency practitioner must be an individual. A firm or a body corporate cannot hold office as an insolvency practitioner. (IA s 390 (1))

5. Certain persons are disqualified from being insolvency practitioners, including undischarged bankrupts, persons disqualified by law and patients under the Mental Health Act 1983. (IA s 390 (4))

6. Only an insolvency practitioner can hold office as:

● a supervisor of a corporate or voluntary arrangement

● an administrator

● an administrative receiver

- a liquidator
- a trustee in bankruptcy. (IA s 388 (1) and (2))

7.   No qualification is required for:

- a Law of Property Act receiver
- a receiver and manager
- a person supervising an informal arrangement.

Corporate Arrangements

What can be achieved by an arrangement?

The possibilities of what can be achieved by an arrangement are almost limitless. For example, the directors of a company which is in difficulties may call the creditors together. They may persuade them that if a formal liquidation were to be entered into, then because of the costs which would be incurred, they would get nothing as unsecured creditors. Accordingly, the creditors are invited to consider the following possible arrangements:

1.   *Offer of lesser sum.* An acceptance by all of them of, say, 20p in the £ in full and final settlement of all debt owing to them by the company.

    Suppose, however, some of the creditors at the meeting feel that the directors themselves should lose something as well. An alternative possibility would be:

2.   The directors would themselves put, say, £50,000 into the fund available for the creditors. This, together with the 20p in the £ from the company described above, would result in the creditors receiving 50p in the £.

    Another possibility would be:

3.   *Debt/equity swap.* Here the creditors would exchange the debts which the company owes to them for fully paid shares in the company. Probably part of the deal offered to the creditors would be that the directors would forfeit their shares and also resign as directors of the company. As a result of such an arrangement the creditors would become the owners of the company. They could then put in a manager. If he could turn the company into profit the

creditors might well then be able to recoup their losses as a result of the company being able to pay them dividends as shareholders or their being able to sell their shares in the company.

Arrangements at common law

1.   In considering arrangements, it should always be remembered that at common law an arrangement agreed to by all creditors is binding.

2.   From elementary contract law, the rule in *Foakes* v *Beer*(1884) 9 App Cas 605 will be remembered. The rule, stated simply, is that a debt must always be paid in full. Payment of a lesser sum will not discharge the debt. However, there are a number of exceptions to the rule. Examples of little practical importance are where the debt is paid in a difference place or in a different currency.

3.   However, two exceptions are of considerable importance in the context of arrangements:

(a) Where all the creditors agree to accept a stated percentage of the debts due to them in full and final settlement of what they are owed: *Wood* v *Robarts* [18 17] 1 Stark 417.

b) Where the debt is paid at a discount by a third party: *Hirachand Punamchand* v *Temple* [1911] 2 KB 330.

(c) The rationale behind these exceptions to the rule in *Foakes* v *Beer* is that to allow a creditor to go behind his agreement to accept a lesser sum in discharge of his debt would be a fraud either upon his fellow creditors or upon the third party paying the debt as the case may be.

4.   As was said above, it is only with a formal arrangement that an insolvency practitioner is needed as the supervisor. Accordingly, if the arrangement is one of these informal arrangements at common law then there is no need to have an insolvency practitioner in charge of it.

5.   In other words, it is only where all the creditors will not agree to the arrangement that a formal procedure is required. This might occur, for example, when a creditor refuses to go along with the arrangement, perhaps because of selfishness, or perhaps because of a desire to see the directors dragged through the courts in a

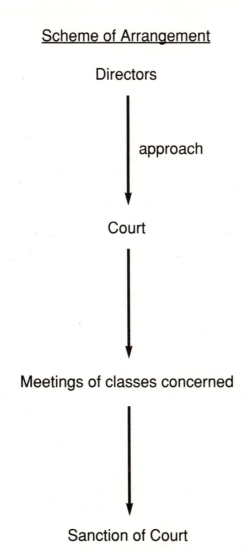

Scheme of Arrangement

Directors

approach

Court

Meetings of classes concerned

Sanction of Court

compulsory liquidation or perhaps because it is the policy of that particular creditor not to accept any form of informal arrangement.

Formal schemes of arrangement

1.   There are two principal ways in which a company can bring about a formal scheme of arrangement:

(a) a scheme of arrangement under the Companies Act 1985 sections 425-427

(b) a corporate voluntary arrangement under Part I of the Insolvency Act 1986.

2.   The section 425 scheme of arrangement has been possible in English law for quite some time. It is, however, rather a cumbersome procedure to bring one about and its repeal was recommended when insolvency law was revised in 1986.

3.   However, this recommendation of repeal was not implemented and it remains on the statute book though it is seldom encountered in the context of corporate insolvency today, its use being mainly confined to matters such as a variation of class rights where those rights have been entrenched in the memorandum of association. For this reason the consideration of schemes of arrangement in this notebook is essentially brief and very much in outline.

4.   The main types of arrangement encountered today in the context of insolvency are corporate voluntary arrangements under Part I of the Insolvency Act 1986 and these are considered in more detail later.

Schemes of arrangement under Companies Act 1985 ss 425-427

1.   A scheme of arrangement is drawn up, usually by way of a document which contains:

(a) an explanatory statement, and

(b) notice of the proposed meeting(s).

2.   The explanatory statement must:

(a) state any material interest of the directors (whether as directors or as members or as creditors of the company) and the effect of the scheme on those arrangements;

(b) if the scheme affects the rights of debenture holders, the statement must give a like explanation as respects the trustees of any debenture trust deed; and

(c) generally explain the effects of the scheme. (CA s 426 (2))

3.   *Application to court.* An application is then made to the court for leave to convene meetings to approve the scheme. The application is made by the company (*ie.* by the directors under their usual power of management) or by the liquidator (if the company is in liquidation). (CA s 425 (1))

4.   The applicant must decide what meetings of creditors and members are necessary. It is then the court that grants an originating summons convening the meetings. The only meetings which will be ordered are those of creditors or members whose rights are affected by the scheme. Thus, if the proposed arrangement were that the creditors would accept, say, 20p in the £, there would be just one meeting, namely of the creditors. On the other hand, if a debt-equity swap were proposed, there would be a meeting of the creditors and also a meeting of the members since their rights will be diluted as a result of the creditors becoming themselves members of the company.

5.   *The hearing,* which is usually before a district judge in chambers, will settle the form of notice of the meetings which is to be sent to the creditors and, if relevant, the members. The judge will also direct that newspaper advertisements should be published if it is possible that individual notices may not reach all intended recipients (for example, where the company has issued share warrants, the holders of whom may be unknown to the company).

6.   The notice sent to the creditors and, if relevant, the members, must be accompanied by the explanatory statement of the scheme referred to above in paragraphs 1 and 2.

7.   *Voting.* Creditors and members entitled to vote at their respective

meetings may do so either in person or by proxy. Forms for appointing proxies will be settled by the judge, but they need not be delivered to the company prior to the meeting. It has been held that it is sufficient that proxy forms are produced at the meeting.

8. At the meetings, the scheme of arrangement must be approved by a composite resolution of both:

   (a) a simple majority in number, and

   (b) three-fourths in value

   of those voting in person or by proxy. (CA s 425(2))

9. If these majorities are obtained, an application may be made to the court for the sanction of the scheme. The court will check that the required meetings have been held and that the necessary resolutions have been properly passed. It will then either give or refuse its sanction to the scheme. It would seem that approval cannot be given subject to conditions. (CA s 425(2))

10. *Report to Registrar.* An office copy of the scheme must then be delivered to the Registrar of Companies. (CA s 425(3))

11. The scheme, so arrived at, is then binding upon all the members and creditors of the company. (CA s 425(2))

12. A copy of the court order must be annexed to every copy of the company's memorandum issued after the order has been made.

Corporate voluntary arrangements

1. As has been said, when insolvency law was being revised in the 1980's, it was a widely held view that the procedures for bringing about a scheme of arrangement under the Companies Act sections 425-427 were too cumbersome and generally unsuitable for a company in serious financial difficulties. For this reason, an alternative procedure was proposed whereby an arrangement could be brought about speedily and without a court order but

nevertheless in circumstances which will make the arrangement binding upon all persons concerned.

2.   The recommended procedure is now to be found in the Insolvency Act 1986 Part I.

A voluntary arrangement in outline

Briefly, the arrangement goes through the following stages.

1.   The directors of the company in difficulties make an approach to an insolvency practitioner (known at this stage as the nominee). (IA s 1(1))

2.   The nominee puts in a report to the court that he feels that an arrangement is possible. (IA s 2(2))

3.   Meetings are called of:

(a) the creditors of the company

(b) the members of the company

to approve the arrangement. (IA s 3(1))

4.   Once the arrangement is approved at these meetings the insolvency practitioner puts in a report of this fact to the court. (IA s 4(6))

5.   The arrangement is then binding upon all those creditors who had a right to attend and to vote at the meeting. (IA s 5(2))

It is vital at this stage to note that the arrangement is only binding upon those creditors having a right to attend and to vote at the meeting. Accordingly it is not binding upon those creditors who did not enjoy this right. Creditors not so bound enjoy all the normal rights of creditors regardless of the arrangement. Thus enormous work could be done in bringing about an arrangement only to see this hard work destroyed by a single creditor emerging after the meeting who, being owed more than £750 and not bound by the arrangement, could then petition for the winding up of the company. For this reason it is vital at the earliest moment (*ie.* ideally before the initial approach is made to the insolvency practitioner) that a comprehensive schedule of all creditors is drawn up and that an approach has been made informally at least to the major creditors to ascertain that they are likely to go along with the proposed arrangement. Often no firm commitment can be obtained, but nevertheless some sense of the creditors' respective views may be obtained.

Voluntary arrangements in detail

1. *Approach to Insolvency practitioner.* So long as the company is not in liquidation or in administration, the directors may at any time commence proceedings for an arrangement under Part I of the Insolvency Act 1986. If, however, the company is in liquidation or is in administration then it is the liquidator or the administrator as the case may be who can initiate the proceedings. (IA ss 2and 3)

2. The proposal to bring about an arrangement made by the directors to an insolvency practitioner, known as the nominee, must contain a short explanation as to why a voluntary arrangement is desirable and why the creditors might be expected to concur in such an arrangement. It must also contain detailed information concerning the assets and liabilities of the company and also give an account of any matters which might arise upon a liquidation, such as transactions adding on a value or preferences made by the company. There must also be sent to the insolvency practitioner details of the proposed arrangement and a statement of affairs. (IR 1.3)

3. *Report to the court.* The nominee must then, within 28 days, report to the court as to whether he feels that the scheme should be considered by the members of the company and by its creditors and, if so when and where meetings of them should be held. (IA s 2(2))

4. If a nominee is unwilling to put in an affirmative report to the court, there appears to be nothing (except lack of funds, time and the

<u>Corporate Voluntary Arrangement</u>

Directors of Debtor Company

approach with proposed arrangement

Insolvency Practitioner (nominee)

report

Court

Meetings
(1) Creditors
(2) Members

Insolvency Practitioner (supervisor)

pressure exerted by creditors) to prevent the directors from generally shopping around to find an insolvency practitioner who is willing to do so.

5. The report to the court is largely a matter of record. The court will not become judicially involved in the procedure unless some problem arises.

6. If the proceedings intended to lead to the implementation of an arrangement are started by a liquidator or by an administrator and he decides that he should himself be the supervisor of the intended arrangement (in other words, he is not going to approach some other insolvency practitioner to be the nominee) then there is no need for him to report to the court. (IA s 3(2))

7. *Calling the meetings.* The next stage in the proceedings is the meetings of the creditors and the members. In the case of the directors having initiated the proceedings, these meetings must be held not less than 14 nor more than 28 days from the nominee's report having been filed in court. (IR 1.9)

8. At least 14 days' notice must be given to both creditors and members of the meetings. (IR 1.9)

9. *Contents of the notice.* The notice must specify the court to which the report was sent by the insolvency practitioner and must state the requisite majority at the creditors' meeting and generally must be accompanied by:

    (a) a copy of the director's proposals

    (b) a copy of the statement of affairs, and

    (c) the nominee's comments on the proposal. (IR 1.9(3))

10. If the proceedings were initiated by a liquidator or administrator, the notice must be accompanied by a copy of his proposal and a statement of affairs. (IR 1.11(2))

11. *The meetings.* Both the creditors' and members' meetings take place on the same day, the creditors' meeting being first (in sharp contrary distinction to the commencement of a creditors' voluntary

liquidation where it is the members' meeting which occurs first). Both meetings must take place between 10.00 and 16.00 hours. In fixing the venue, regard must be had by the nominee to the convenience of the creditors. (IR 1.13)

12. Of the two meetings, the creditors' meeting is obviously the crucial one. Since the directors are likely also to be the members of the company, the outcome of the members' meeting is usually a foregone conclusion.

13. *Voting.* At the creditors' meeting, any resolution for approving or modifying an arrangement must be passed by a majority in excess of three-quarters in value of the creditors voting in person or by proxy. (IR 1.19)

14. Any other resolution requires a majority in excess of one-half in value of the creditors. (IR 1.19(2))

15. *Connected persons.* It will, however, be appreciated that often when a company is in difficulties a major creditor will be someone such as a director who has himself advanced money to the company to try to keep it afloat and as such would claim on a liquidation claim as an unsecured creditor. Logically, it would be unfair for an arrangement to be steamrollered through as a result of debts owed to a director or some similarly connected person if a majority of the "independent creditors" were against the arrangement.

16. For this reason, any resolution is invalid if those persons voting against it include more than one-half in value of creditors who are not connected with the company. (IR 1.19(4))

17. A person is connected with the company if:

(a) he is a director or a shadow director of the company or an associate of such a director or shadow director, or

(b) he is an associate of the company. (IA s 249)

18. *Shadow director.* A shadow director means a person in accordance with whose directions or instructions the directors of the company are accustomed to act, though not a person merely giving advice in a professional capacity. (IA s 251)

19. *Associate.* An associate of an individual means that an individual's husband or wife, or a relative of the individual, or a relative of such husband or wife, or the husband or wife of any such relative. (IA s 435)

20. A relative means a brother, sister, uncle, aunt, nephew, niece, lineal ancestor or lineal descendant. Relationships of the half blood are treated as relationships of the whole blood. Stepchildren and adopted children are treated as children of the whole blood. (IA s 435)

21. A company is an associate of another company:

(a) if the same person has control of both, or a person has control of one and persons who are his associates have control of the other, or

(b) if a group of two or more persons has control of each company, and the groups either consist of the same persons or could be regarded as consisting of the same persons by treating a member of either group as replaced by a person of whom he is an associate.(IA s 435)

22. *Secured and preferential creditors.* An arrangement cannot affect the rights of any secured or preferential creditor unless that creditor specifically agrees the variation. (IA s 4(3))

23. Secured creditors cannot vote in respect of any part of their debt which is secured. (IR 1.19(3)(c))

24. *Chairman's powers.* The chairman of the meeting is usually the nominee, but sometimes may be a senior employee of the nominee having insolvency experience (IR 1.14). The chairman has complete discretion whether to remit or reject the claim of any creditor for the purpose of his entitlement to vote. This power is exerciseable in respect of all or part of any creditor's claim. Thus it is open to a chairman to say to a creditor who claims to be owed £10,000 that he does not believe the claim and will only permit him to vote for, say, £4,000. In these circumstances, the creditor will still be entitled to have his disallowed vote recorded in the minutes of the meeting. This may be useful to him in the event of his appealing the outcome of the meeting. (IR 1.17(4))

25. *The meetings.* The creditors' and members' meeting must be held on the same day and at the same place. The creditors' meeting is, however, always the first to be held. (IR 1.13)

26. As has been said, the creditors' meeting must agree the proposed arrangement by a vote of more than three-quarter in value of those creditors attending or voting by proxy. (IR 1.19(1))

27. At the members' meeting, unless there is some contrary provision in the articles of the company, any resolution is passed by more than one-half in value of those members voting in person or by proxy. The value of members is determined by reference to the number of votes conferred by each member by the company's articles of association. (IR 1.18)

28. *Effect of approval.* Once each of the meetings has approved the arrangement, it takes effect as if made by the company at the creditors' meeting (in other words it backdates to the creditors' meeting even though the successful outcome is not certain until the members' meeting has been held). It then becomes binding on every person who had notice of, and was entitled to vote at that meeting. This is so whether he actually voted or not. The converse of this is, of course, that the arrangement is not binding upon any creditor who did not have notice of the meeting. (IA s 5)

29. The nominee now becomes the supervisor of the arrangement (unless some other insolvency practitioner was appointed to the post at the meetings (IA s 7). The directors must do all that is necessary to put him into possession of the assets included in the arrangement. (IR 1.23)

30. *The report.* The chairman of the meetings must prepare a report stating whether the proposal for the voluntary arrangement was approved or rejected (IA s 4(6)). This report must also set out the resolutions passed at each meeting, listing the creditors and members and showing how they voted. The report must be filed in court within four days of the conclusion of the meetings. Notice of the result of the meetings must then be given to all persons to whom notice of the meetings was given. A copy of the chairman's report must also be sent to the Registrar of Companies. (IR 1.24)

31. *Power of the court.* If an arrangement takes effect at a time when the

company is in liquidation or administration, the court may:

(a) stay all proceedings in the winding up or discharge of the administration order; or

(b) give such directions with respect to the conduct of the winding up or the administration as it thinks appropriate for facilitating the implementation of the approved voluntary arrangement. (IA s 5)

32. *Appeal.* An appeal may be lodged against the implementation of a voluntary arrangement within 28 days of the filing in court of the reports by the chairman of the meetings. The appeal may be on the grounds either that:

(a) it unfairly prejudices the interests of a creditor, a member or a contributory of the company, or

(b) there has been some material irregularity at or in relation to either of the meetings. (IA s 6)

33. The persons who are entitled to appeal are:

(a) any person entitled to vote at either of the meetings

(b) the nominee or any person appointed to replace him

(c) if the company is in liquidation or administration, the liquidator or the administrator of the company.

34. Upon such an appeal being heard, the court may revoke or suspend the approvals given by the meetings and/or give a direction to any person for the summoning of further meetings to consider any revised proposal the person making the original proposal may make.

35. *Ultimate sanction.* Inevitably any arrangement is going to depend upon promises being kept, for example promises by the directors that they will pay a specified amount to the supervisor to be divided amongst the creditors of the company. If such promises are not kept, then the supervisor is one of the people who has *locus standi* to apply to the court for a winding up order in respect of the company. (IA s 7(4))

Administration Orders

Introduction

1. The nature of the administration order is perhaps best illustrated by considering first the nature of execution of a judgment.

2. Execution is essentially a matter of self-help for a creditor. For example, a supplier of goods, immediately after making a delivery, submits an invoice to his customer. So soon as the period of grace on the invoice has expired, he immediately takes proceedings in the county court for judgment. So soon as it becomes obvious that the judgment debt is not going to be paid he seeks execution. In its simplest terms, this means that a bailiff will go to the premises of the debtor and seize sufficient goods, the proceeds of sale of which will satisfy the judgment. In general terms as soon as the goods have been sold the proceeds of sale are available for the judgment creditor and are accordingly lost to the generality of the creditors of the debtor. In other words, execution is a form of self-help by a creditor.

3. So long as the debtor is not in a state of formal insolvency, there is no reason why such self-help should not be practised by individual creditors who have their wits about them. However, once a debtor is in a state of formal insolvency, that debtor's assets must be ring-fenced so as to be available for the creditors in the order laid down by law. This concept of ring-fencing the assets of a debtor is easily enough accepted when one considers a company in liquidation or in administrative receivership.

4.   However, consider the situation of a company which is not in liquidation or in administrative receivership but where its directors are trying to achieve an arrangement amongst the creditors. The arrangement could be totally destroyed if individual creditors could receive assets of the company by way of self-help as described above.

5.   For this reason, in 1986 the administration order was introduced. This is an order of the court which has the effect of temporarily ring-fencing the assets of the company while the directors try to work out some rescue strategy for the company. It is essentially of a short term nature and, unlike all other insolvency procedures, is not an end in itself but merely a transitional stage leading to something else.

6.   Throughout any consideration of administration orders, it is essential to bear in mind that the nature of the order is to hold back the creditors of the company while something is being worked out.

Procedure for applying for an administration arder

1.   *Petitioners.* An application for an administration order may be made either by the company or by its directors or by a creditor or a group of its creditors. Usually the application is made by the directors. (IA s 9)

2.   It is interesting to note that there are a number of people who could apply for a winding up order who have no *locus standi* to apply for an administration order. For example, the Official Receiver cannot apply for an administration order, nor can the Secretary of State. Likewise an individual member cannot apply for an order, which is in sharp contradistinction to the power of a member to petition for the winding up on the just and equitable ground or for relief from unfair prejudice under the Companies Act section 459.

3.   *Ground.* The application for an administration order must establish two things:

      • that the company is, or is likely to become, unable to pay its debts; and

- that the order is likely to achieve one of the following:-

(a)   the survival of the company in whole or in part

(b)   the sanctioning of an arrangement under the Companies Act section 425

(c)   the approval of a voluntary arrangement under Part I of the Insolvency Act 1986

(d)   the more advantageous realisation of the company's assets than would be achieved on a formal winding up. (IA s 8(3))

4.   *Nature of administration order.* The nature of an administration order can perhaps be illustrated by considering the facts of two cases:

Re Consumer & Industrial Press Limited [1988] 4 BCC 68

The company was a small printing and publishing house. It was heavily insolvent. Its only asset of any value was the magazine title *Pins and Needles*. As will be seen, an administrator has power, like an administrative receiver, to borrow so as to continue the business of the company. An administration order was granted so that the administrator could continue publishing the magazine, so that he could ultimately sell the title as a going concern. In other words, it was hoped that he would achieve a more advantageous realisation of the company's assets than would be achieved on a formal winding up.

Re Newport County Association Football Club Limited [1987] 3 BCC 635

The football club was very seriously insolvent. There was a possibility of a voluntary arrangement being made with the creditors, probably by way of a debt-equity swap. The administration order was made in the hope that an arrangement could be arrived at.

5.   *Affidavit.* The petition to the court for an administration order must be accompanied by an affidavit which must contain the following:

(a) a statement of the company's financial position, specifying its assets and liabilities including contingent and prospective liabilities

(b) details of any security held by creditors of the company and stating whether there is any power to appoint an administrative receiver and whether an administrative receiver has been appointed

(c) details of any winding up petition presented against the company

(d) details of any other matters which the persons presenting the petition believe may be of assistance to the court

(e) a statement of whether an independent report has been prepared for the company, and, if not, why not. (IR 2.3)

6.   *Independent report.* The independent report referred to is one made usually by the person who it is intended should be the administrator of the company. The report should state that the appointment of an administrator is expedient. Alternatively, the report may be made by some other person having an adequate knowledge of the company's affairs, so long as he is not a director, secretary, manager, member or employee of the company. (IR 2.2)

7.   *Notice to holder of floating charge.* A copy of the petition and the accompanying affidavit must be served on any person who has appointed, or is or may be entitled to appoint an administrative receiver (IA s 9(2)). As will be seen shortly, an administrative receiver is a receiver appointed under a floating charge which itself is over the whole or substantially the whole of the undertaking of the company. A creditor most likely to have such a floating charge permitting him to appoint an administrative receiver is the company's bank. So that they can be made aware of any application of any administration order, banks today invariably take a floating charge over the undertaking of their customer companies whether or not they need such security in strictly commercial terms. Five days' notice must be given to the person entitled to appoint the administrative receiver though this can be truncated by order of the court in the event of there being a need for the administration order to be made the more quickly. (see *eg.* Re a Company N° 00175 of 1987 (1987) 3 BCC 124.)

8.   *Notice to sheriff.* Notice must also be given by the petitioner to:

(a) any sheriff or other officer who to his knowledge is charged with an execution or other legal process against the company or its property

(b) any person who to his knowledge has disclaimed against the company or its property. (IR 2.6A)

9. There is generally no need to give notice to any other person. Indeed, since the intention is that an administration order should be speedily made, there is no time and indeed no requirement for the application to be Gazetted or otherwise advertised.

10. *Effect of petition.* The effect of the presentation of the petition is to bring about an immediate moratorium in all creditor actions and other remedies against the company. In more detail, this means that:

(a) there can be no winding up resolution passed and no winding up order made in respect of the company

(b) there can be no steps taken to enforce any security over the company's property, or to repossess goods in the possession of the company under any hire-purchase agreement, except with the leave of the court. In this regard references to higher purchase include conditional sale agreements, chattel leasing agreements and retention of title agreements.

(c) there can be no other proceedings and no execution or other legal process may be commenced or continued, and no distress may be levied against the company or its property, except with the leave of the court. (IA s 10)

11. *Creditor rights.* However, there are two creditor rights which can be pursued without the leave of the court.

(a) a petition for the winding up of the company may be presented

(b) an administrative receiver may be appointed. (IA s 10(2))

12. If a winding up petition is presented, it is likely to be heard in tandem with the petition for the administration order. If the application for the administration order is successful, the winding up petition will be dismissed (IA s 11(1)(a)). On the other hand, if the application for the administration order fails, the winding up petition is likely to be successful.

13. *Appointment of administrative receiver.* If an administrative receiver is appointed by the time that the petition is heard, the petition must

Procedure on Presentation of Petition

Petition (usually presented by directors)

Notice → Any person entitled to appoint administrative receiver (usually the bank)

↓

Pre-emptive appointment of administrative receiver

↓

Petition for administration order dismissed

be dismissed unless either:

(a) the person who appointed the administrative receiver gives his consent to the administration order, or

(b) the administrative receiver had been appointed under a floating charge which was potentially void, for example because of non-registration under the Companies Act section 395. (IA s 9(3))

14. *Power of the bank.* Thus it will be appreciated that if the bank having a floating charge over the undertaking of a company makes a pre-emptive appointment of an administrative receiver as soon as it is told of an application for an administration order then the administration cannot be made. In other words the one creditor who must be told of the application for the administration order is the one person who can prevent it from being made.

15. *Standard of proof.* Before making an administration order, the court must be satisfied that it will be "likely to achieve" the purpose specified in the petition. This means that it must be more likely than not that it will be achieved. A mere possibility that it may be achieved is not sufficient. See *eg.Re Harris Simons Construction Ltd* (1989) 5 BCC 11, *Re Primlaks (UK) Ltd* (1989) 5 BCC 710 and *Re SCL Building Services Ltd* (1989) 5 BCC 746.

16. *Costs.* If an application for an administration order is dismissed and a winding up order is made, the costs incurred for the abortive application for the administration order will normally be liable as an expense of the winding up so long as the court is satisfied that the directors acted in good faith in making the application and that their conduct generally was reasonable: see *eg. Re Gosscott (Groundworks) Ltd* (1988)4 BCC 372. On the other hand it must be appreciated that since an application for an administration order can be abused by directors of a company which is in difficulties merely to try to buy more time for themselves, the liability of costs in this way is not automatic.

17. *Procedure following order.* Following the making of an administration order, the administrator must advertise the order:

(a) once in the *Gazette* and

(b) once in such newspapers as he thinks most appropriate for ensuring that the order comes to the notice of the company's creditors.

He must also give notice to any person who has appointed or has power to appoint an administrative receiver, to any person who has presented a winding up petition and to the Registrar of Companies. (IR 2.10)

18. When an administration order is made, any administrative receiver who is in post must vacate office. Moreover, the administrator can require any other receivers of any part of the company's property to vacate office. (IA s 11)

19. *Effect of the order.* The effect of the order is to continue the moratorium begun by the presentation of the petition. Thus, for so long as the order is in force, there can by:

(a) no resolution passed or order made for the winding up of the company

(b) no appointment of any administrative receiver

(c) no other steps taken to enforce any security over the property of the company or to repossess goods in the possession of the company under any hire-purchase agreement, including goods on hire or subject to any other legal proceedings, execution, distress or other legal process unless the consent is obtained either of the administrator or of the court. (IA s 10(1))

20. On the other hand, the moratorium is essentially only in respect of creditor rights against the company. Therefore legal proceedings can be taken against the company by persons who are not creditors. For example, in one case the CAA was permitted to bring proceedings against a company in administration for the revocation of an air transport licence: *Air Ecosse Ltd* v *Civil Aviation Authority* (1987) 3 BCC 492.

21. While the company is in administration, its stationery must state this to be the case and give the name of the administrator. (IA s 12)

The powers of the administrator

1. As has been said any creditor having a floating charge over the whole or substantially the whole of the undertaking of the company (usually the company's bankers) must be given notice of the application for the administration order. That floating charge holder then has a right to block the appointment of the administrator by making a pre-emptive appointment of an administrative receiver which prevents the court from appointing an administrator. Such a pre-emptive appointment is invariably made and this results in there being very few administration orders ever made in practice. A major reason why administration orders are not made is because of the vast power wielded by the administrator. The next four paragraphs detail these precise powers.

2. The administrator enjoys the same powers, set out in Schedule 1 to the, Insolvency Act 1986 as the administrative receiver. These include the power to

    - take possession of all property of the company

    - sell property of the company

    - raise money on security

    - carry on the business of the company

    - appoint agents

    - execute documents and deeds in the name of the company

    - use the company's seal.

    Suppose, a bank having a floating charge over the undertaking of the company were faced with the possibility of having an administrator to wield these powers or an administrative receiver, over whom it would have some control, it is perhaps obvious that the bank would rather have its own person, the administrative receiver, wielding the powers.

3. *Control of directors.* The administrator can appoint and remove directors and can call meetings of both members and creditors of the company (IA s14(2)). In other words the administrator is subrogated

to the position of the general meeting of the company and could, at least in theory, entirely change the constitution of the board of the company without let or hinderance from anyone.

4. *Property subject to floating charge.* The administrator can dispose of or otherwise exercise his powers in relation to any property of the company which is subject to a floating charge as if the property were not subject to that security (IA s 15(1)). In this regard the administrator is in a similar position to the board of directors of the company. They, too, can dispose of property subject to a floating charge as though the property were not subject to that security (IA s 15(1)). However, in the event of a bank forming the view that the directors were dissipating the assets of the company, they could immediately call a halt to such conduct by appointing an administrative receiver. However, if it were an administrator who was exercising these powers, the bank having a floating charge would be powerless, since, it would be recalled, so long as an administrator is in post, an administrative receiver cannot be appointed.

5. *Property subject to other security.* The administrator can dispose of any other property subject to any other security with the consent of the court if he can satisfy the court that the disposal would be likely to promote the achievement of the purpose of the administration order. When making such an order, the court can act as though the property were not subject to any security rights (IA s 15(2)). Thus, for example, suppose a bank had a fixed charge over a warehouse owned by a company. The company goes into administration, with the administrator being appointed to achieve the survival of the company. The administrator forms a view that the survival can be best achieved by selling the warehouse and moving into smaller rented accommodation. Accordingly he applies to the court for an order to sell the warehouse. The bank objects. The bank's objection is disregarded by the court and an order for sale is made. The warehouse is auctioned and realises far less than the administrator had hoped. Indeed there is now a negative equity situation. The bank could have prevented this situation from arising if, as well as the fixed charge over the warehouse, it had also taken a floating charge over the remainder of the undertaking of the company. This would have given it power to appoint an administrative receiver upon being given notice of the application for an administration

order and such appointment would have prevented the making of the administration order.

6.   *Newly acquired property.* If property is disposed of which is subject to a floating charge, the holder of the security has the same priority in respect of any property of the company directly or indirectly representing the property disposed of as he would have have in respect of the property subject to the security (IA s 15(1)). In other words, where the administrator disposes of property subject to a floating charge and the company purchases or otherwise acquires other property coming within the generic description of property charged by the floating charge, then that property also falls under the floating charge.   Thus, the administrator is in exactly the same position as the board of directors of a going concern company. He can dispose of property subject to a floating charge and when the company acquires more of such property that in turn falls under the charge.

7.   *Rights of Secured Creditor.* If property is disposed of which is subject to any other form of security, the court must order that the proceeds of the sale shall be applied in discharging the sum secured by the security. Thus, in the example given above, if the bank were to order the sale of a warehouse subject to a fixed charge, the repayment of the fixed charge would be a first priority from the proceeds of sale obtained.

The conduct of the administration

1.   *Agency of Administrator.* The administrator is deemed to be the agent of the company. (IA s 14(5))

2.   Any person dealing with an administrator in good faith and value is not concerned to enquire whether he is acting within his powers. (IA s 14(6))

3.   Upon appointment, the administrator must take into his custody or control all the property to which the company is or appears to be entitled. (IA s 17(1))

4. Obviously the administrator must manage the affairs of the company in accordance with any instructions given to him by the court. (IA s 17(2))

5. The administrator will have been appointed for a specific purpose, namely to achieve the survival of the company, or to bring about a scheme of arrangement, or to bring about a voluntary arrangement, or to achieve a better realisation of the assets than would be obtained on a formal winding up. If at any time he forms the view that the purpose for which he was appointed cannot be achieved, he must apply to the court for the order to be discharged. (IA s 18(2))

6. *Information to creditors.* Within three months of the making of the administration order, or such longer period as the court may allow, the administrator must send to the Registrar of Companies and to all the creditors of the company a statement of his proposals for achieving the purpose for which he was appointed. (IA s 23(1))

7. He must also within this time period send a copy to all the members of the company. (IA s 23(2))

8. He must then call a meeting of the company's creditors for them to decide whether to approve the administrator's proposals. (IA ss23 and 24)

9. Following a meeting, the administrator must report the result of the meeting to the court and to the Registrar of Companies. He must also send notice of the result of the meeting to every creditor to whom notice of the meeting was given. (IA s 24(4) and IR 2.30)

10. If the creditors wish for some on-going control over the administrator, they may, at this meeting, establish a creditors' committee. The committee must consist of any three, four or five creditors. Its function is to assist the administrator in the discharge of his duties and to act in relation to him in such manner as may be agreed from time to time. (IA s 26)

11. Having completed the administration, the administrator must apply to the court for his discharge. Such a release discharges him from all liability both in respect of acts or omissions of his in the administration and otherwise in relation to his conduct as administrator. (IA s 20)

Receivers

Introduction

1. A debenture holder is a creditor of the company. Although in commercial circles there appears to be an assumption generally that a debenture is secured, this is not necessarily the case. There is no statutory definition of a debenture. The classic definition is that of Chitty J in *Levy* v *Abercorris Slate and Slab Co* [1887] 37 Ch D 260 where he described a debenture as "a document with either creates a debt or acknowledges it".

2. There is thus no need for a debenture to be secured. It may be unsecured or "naked".

3. The difference between the secured and the unsecured debenture holder lies in the remedies available to him.

4. *Remedies of unsecured debenture holder.* The holder of an unsecured debenture has two remedies. He may sue for the money or, so long as he is owed more than £750, he may petition for the winding up of the company.

5. If he sues successfully for the money, he can then obtain execution on the judgment debt.

6. There may be no great advantage to the holder of an unsecured debenture petitioning for the winding up of a company since in the liquidation he will merely rank as an unsecured creditor along with

all the other unsecured creditors of the company.

7. *Remedies of secured debenture holder.* The holder of a secured debenture enjoys these remedies though rarely will he rely upon them. In addition to them, he also may appoint a receiver if permitted to do so under the terms of the debenture or apply to the court for the appointment of a receiver if the debenture is silent in this regard.

Appointment of receivers by the court

1. Traditionally, the Court of Chancery had an inherent jurisdiction to appoint a receiver where such an appointment was necessary for the purposes of justice.

2. Following the Supreme Court of Judicature Act 1873, this jurisdiction is now enjoyed by any division of the High Court.

3. *Role of receivers.* There are two main categories of case where the court traditionally makes the appointment of a receiver:

   (a) where the appointment is necessary to allow persons having rights over property to exercise those rights and to ensure the preservation of the property until it can be realised

   (b) where the appointment is necessary to preserve the property from some danger which is threatening it.

4. *LPA receivers.* A typical example of where a receiver might traditionally be appointed is where a lender has lent to a landlord on the security of tenanted property. The landlord defaults on the mortgage and the lender applies to the court for the appointment of a receiver. The appointment is on terms that in future the rent will be paid by the tenants to the receiver and the receiver will discharge the landlord's obligations as borrower to the lender. Logically there is no reason why such a commonplace appointment of a receiver as this should have to be done by the court and today such an appointment is usually made out of court under the Law of Property Act 1925.

5.   However, the court still retains its inherent jurisdiction to appoint a receiver. Examples of such appointment are:

Court appointed receivers

Re Oakes [1917] 1 Ch 230

> This was a probate matter. Action was proceeding between a beneficiary and the named executor. An appointment of a receiver was made over the property of the deceased pending the outcome of the action.

Re Clark [1910] WN 131

> Again this was a probate matter. A sole executor died without having himself appointed an executor. A receiver was appointed pending the appointment of an administrator.

Re Compton and Co Limited [1914] Ch 954

> A receiver was appointed where a company was in liquidation.

> Incidentally, this highlights the role of the receiver. He is essentially appointed to look after the interests of the secured creditor by whom he is appointed. Thus when a company goes into liquidation, a receiver may be, and usually is, appointed by a secured debenture holder to look after his narrower interests as against the wider interests to which the liquidator must have regard.

Hart v Emelkirk Limited [1983] 3 All ER 15

> Tenants of a privately owned block of flats were dissatisfied with the care which their landlord was taking of the block. Accordingly they applied to the court for the appointment of a receiver to whom they should pay the rent. The receiver would then ensure the proper maintenance of the flats.

Law of Property Act Receivers

Receiver

1. By section 101 of the Law of Property Act, a mortgagee under a mortgage created by a deed may appoint a receiver to receive the income of the mortgage property.

2. *Appointment.* This power is, however, only exercisable if one of three conditions is satisfied:

(a) the mortgagor must have been served with a notice requiring payment of the mortgage money and three months must have elapsed during which payment has not been made in full

(b) interest due under the mortgage agreement must be two months in arrears, or

(c) there must have been some other breach of the mortgage agreement.

3. The appointment must be made in writing. (LPA s 109(1))

4. The appointment takes affect when the document appointing the receiver has been handed to the receiver and he has accepted the appointment: *Cripps (Pharmeceuticals) Ltd* v *Wickenden* [1973] 2 All ER 606.

5. *When court needed.* Generally the appointment is out of court. However, if there is action pending between the mortgagor and the mortgagee, an application should be made to the court for the appointment of a receiver.

6. *Powers of receiver.* The receiver appointed under this provision has power only to receive the income of the mortgaged property. Thus, unless there is some extension of this statutory power, the receiver has no power to sell the property.

7. *Agency.* The receiver is deemed to be the agent of the mortgagor, and the mortgagor is solely responsible for the acts of the receiver unless the mortgage deed provides to the contrary. (LPA s 109(2))

Powers of the Law of Property Act receiver

The receiver has the following powers:

1. *Power to demand and to recover all the income of which he is appointed receiver, by action, by distress or otherwise.* (LPA s 109 (s))

2. *Power of sale.* As has been said in the previous note, the LPA receiver does not, without more power, have the power of sale. The power of sale will only occur in three situations:

    (a) where there is an express power in the mortgage deed

    (b) where the power of sale is exercised in circumstances where the mortgage money has become due and the receiver is exercising the mortgagee's right of sale

    (c) where an application has been made to the court and the court has granted the receiver the power of sale.

3. *Power to insure.* This power is primarily enjoyed by the mortgagee but it may be delegated by him to the receiver.

4. *Power to grant leases.* A mortgagee has power to grant leases of up to 21 years in the case of agricultural or occupation leases and up to 99 years in the case of building leases. This power may be delegated to a receiver.

5. *Power to accept surrender of leases.* Again this power, enjoyed by a mortgagee, can be delegated to a receiver.

Removal of Law of Property Act receivers

A receiver appointed under the Law of Property Act can be removed via the mortgagee by notice in writing.

Remuneration of Law of Prperty Act receiver

1. The receiver may obtain remuneration from any monies received by him.

2. In addition to costs he may receive commission of not more than 5% of all monies received by him. This should be specified in the terms of his appointment.

3. The receiver may apply to the court for permission to charge commission at some higher rate should this be necessary.

Application of monies received

1. Monies received by a Law of Property Act receiver must be applied in the following order:

   (a) in discharging rents, rates and taxes

   (b) in keeping down interest on the principal sum payable on any prior mortgage

   (c) in payment of the receiver's commission and of premiums on fire, life and other insurances which are properly payable under the terms of the mortgage or under the Law of Property Act and the cost of carrying out any necessary repairs directed in writing by the mortgagee

   (d) in payment of the interest accruing due in respect of the principal sum due under the mortgage

(e) in the discharge of the principal money if so directed by the mortgagee in writing. (LPA s 109 (8))

2.   *Residue.* Any residue remaining in the hands of the receiver after the payment of the above should then be paid to the person who, but for the appointment of the receiver, would be entitled to the income from the mortgage property. (LPA s 109 (8))

3.   *Creditors' rights.* The receiver's obligation to discharge liabilities in this order of priority is a duty owed only to the mortgagor and the mortgagee. Thus, a prospective payee, for example HM Customs and Excise in respect of VAT due, had no *locus standi* to bring proceedings to enforce payment by a receiver: see *Re John Willment (Ashford) Ltd* [1979] 2 All ER 615.

4.   Failure to make the due payment may result in the receiver being sued by the mortgagor or by the mortgagee for loss caused by such failure: see *Re John Willment (Ashford) Ltd, ibid*

Administrative Receivers

Introduction

1. *Types of security.* The security given in a debenture can take one of two forms. It may be a fixed charge. Alternatively it may be a floating charge.

2. *Fixed change.* A fixed charge is usually attached to a fixed asset, such as an office block or a warehouse belonging to the company.

3. *Floating charge.* A floating charge, on the other hand, is attached merely to a class of assets which, of their nature, the directors must be free to deal with on a day to day basis. Assets on which a floating charge may be fixed include things such as raw materials, work in progress, finished products, etc.

4. The floating charge was recognised by the courts in the late nineteenth century. When problems arose the courts would appoint a receiver to administer the assets subject to a floating charge, perhaps because a receiver would have been appointed in like circumstances under a fixed charge. However, the floating charge receiver is completely different from a fixed charge receiver. A fixed charge receiver is appointed literally to receive income and little more. On the other hand, the assets on which the floating charge is secured, for example work in progress, have little inherent value until it is completed. Accordingly the floating charge receiver would have to be something of an accountant/businessman who would run the business, complete the work in progress and sell off the finished products.

5. *Adminstrative receivers.* In 1986 the difference between the receiver appointed under a floating charge and that appointed under a fixed charge was recognised by the requirement that the floating charge receiver was generally to be known as an administrative receiver and would have in future to be an insolvency practitioner. (IA s 388)

6. An administrative receiver is defined as a receiver or manager of the whole or substantially the whole of the property of the company appointed by or on behalf of the holders of any debentures secured on creation by a floating charge (IA s 29(2)). Thus there are two elements to the definition:

   (a) he is appointed by or on behalf of the debenture holders. This means he cannot be appointed by the court. The expression "on behalf of" refers to the situation where there has been a flotation of debenture stock under which there is a debenture trust deed appointing trustees representing the interests of the individual lenders and who appoint a receiver on their behalf in the event of default.

   (b) the floating charge must be over the whole or substantially the whole of the undertaking of the company.

7. It is, of course, easy to think of a manufacturing company trading from a single site. Here, any floating charge taken as security by its bankers would inevitably be over the whole or substantially the whole of the undertaking of the company. However, it is all too easy to assume that a floating charge is always going to be over the whole or substantially the whole of the undertaking of the company. But this is not so. For example, to a building company, land is more of the nature of a raw material rather than a fixed asset. Thus, land owned by a building company will often be subject to a floating rather than a fixed charge so that the directors can sell finished plots as the houses are completed. A building company will develop a site, or even part of the site by an individual floating charge. Such a floating charge would not be over the whole or substantially the whole of the undertaking of the company.

8. *Types of receiver.* As has been said, it is only the administrative receiver who has to be an insolvency practitioner. A receiver and manager appointed under a floating charge which is not over the whole or substantially the whole of the undertaking of a company

need not be an insolvency practitioner.

Thus there are three types of receiver:

(a) a Law of Property Act receiver or some similar court appointed receiver whose role is basically to receive income

(b) an administrative receiver appointed under a floating charge which is over the whole or substantially the whole of the undertaking of the company

(c) a receiver and the manager under any other sort of floating charge.

9.   It is very easy for a property developer to assume that a receiver appointed by him will be a receiver and manager rather than an administrative receiver and therefore need not be an insolvency practitioner.   However, care must be taken in making the appointment of the receiver particularly in the case of a single site development where a developer is developing only one site through a company which has issued a floating charge. Almost inevitably this floating charge is going to be over the whole or substantially the whole of the undertaking of the company and therefore a receiver appointed in this instance will be an administrative receiver and therefore must be an insolvency practitioner.

Appointment of the administrative receiver

1.   A properly drafted secure debenture will give express power for the chargee to appoint a receiver.

2.   *Demand.* Before a receiver can be appointed, the chargee must make a demand for repayment of the outstanding debt.

3.   The form of the demand depends on the construction of the debenture.   Often the debenture will require the demand to be in writing. The demand should state the amount due but, since there frequently is some dispute between the charger and the chargee as to the amount due, the correctness of the amount stated is not a condition precedent to a valid demand.

4. If a security instrument simply secures "all monies owing", the demand may similarly be expressed in this way rather than state the specific amount due.

5. *Conflicting interests.* As in so many instances in practice, when a chargee is seeking to enforce his security a balance must be struck between the interests of the parties in conflict. On the one hand, the company must have an opportunity of rescuing itself from its difficulties. On the other hand, the chargee must be able to protect its position as lender to the company in difficulties. Clearly these two conflicting interests are irreconcileable. Accordingly, the approach of the law is that the company has had its chance and it is now the chargee which can protect itself. Accordingly, the demand should merely give the directors a reasonable time to make the repayment. What is a reasonable time depends upon the circumstances. In *Cripps (Pharmaceuticals) Limited* v *Wickenden* [1973] 2 All ER 606 it was held that a demand made at 10.45 am gave sufficient notice to permit the chargee to appoint a receiver at 2.15 pm.

6. Once the demand has been served, the appointment is made in writing by the chargee. The appointment must be accepted by the receiver before the end of the next business day. The acceptance must then be confirmed in writing by the receiver by seven days. (IA s 33 and IR 3.1(2))

It should be noted that the appointment of the receiver is by the chargee. Newsreaders and journalists, for some unknown reason, seem very keen to refer to a company "calling in" the receivers. This, of course, is complete tripe. Sometimes the directors of the company which is in difficulties will approach a bank and ask it to appoint a receiver in the hope that someone of commercial credibility, such as the receiver, will be able to restore its fortunes. However, even here the appointment depends upon the bank being willing to act in accordance with the directors' wishes rather than the company calling in the receiver. In many cases, on the other hand, the bank having the floating charge will not wish to give the directors any longer than the absolute minimum amount of notice of the impending appointment of the receiver for fear that the directors will dispose in some way of assets subject to the floating charge.

7.   *Procedure on appointment.* The administrative receiver must immediately upon appointment give notice to the company. (IA s 46(1))

8.   Notice of the appointment must then be given by the debenture holder to the Registrar of Companies within seven days of the appointment. (CA s 405)

9.   The administrative receiver must publish a notice of his appointment in the *London Gazette* and also in such newspapers as he thinks most appropriate for ensuring that it comes to the notice of the company's creditors. (IA s 46(1) and IR 3.2)

10.   The administrative receiver must require the directors to submit to him a statement of affairs. Within 21 days of receiving this request, the directors must comply with it. (IA s 47)

11.   The administrative receiver must give notice within 28 days of his appointment to all the creditors of the company unless the court directs otherwise. (IA s 46(1))

12.   *Receiver's report.* Within three months of his appointment, the administrative receiver must prepare a report detailing the following:

(a) the events leading to his appointment

(b) the disposal or proposed disposal by him of any property of the company and the carrying on or proposed carrying on by him of any business of the company

(c) the amounts of principal and interest payable to the debenture holders by whom or on whose behalf he was appointed and the amounts payable to preferential creditors, and

(d) the amount, if any, likely to be available for the payment of the other creditors. (IA s 48)

13.   This report must be sent to the Registrar of Companies, any trustees who may have been appointed under the debenture and all unsecured creditors.(IA s 48(1))

14.   The administrative receiver must then, on giving not less than 14

days notice, call a meeting of the unsecured creditors for the purpose of considering the report. (IA s 48(2))

15. If it thinks fit, the meeting may establish a creditors' committee. If established, the committee must consist of three, four or five creditors. Its function is to assess the administrative receiver in discharging his functions, and to act in relation to him in such manner as may be agreed from time to time. On giving seven days' notice, the committee can require the administrative receiver to attend before it at any reasonable time and give it such information as to what he has been doing in the receivership as it may reasonable require. (IA s 49, IR 3.16 and 3.18)

Powers of the administrative receiver

1. The powers of the administrative receiver, like those of the administrator, are set out in Schedule I, Insolvency Act 1986. Thus he has power to take possession of the property of the company, to sell property of the company, to raise money on security, to carry on the business of the company, to appoint agents, to execute documents and deeds in the name of the company and to use the company's seal. (IA s 42(1))

2. These powers are exerciseable by the administrative receiver except in so far as they are inconsistent with any provision in the debenture under which he was appointed. (IA s 42(1))

3. No such powers are given to a receiver and manager by the Act. Accordingly, his powers are to be found in the terms of his appointment or the debenture under which he was appointed.

4. *Rights of third party.* A person who deals with an administrative receiver in good faith and value is not concerned to enquire whether the receiver is acting within his powers. (IA s 42(3))

5. An administrative receiver may apply to the court for an order allowing him to sell property subject to a charge ranking in priority to the charge under which he was appointed. The net proceeds from

the sale must be applied in discharging the prior security. (IA s 43)

Agency of the administrative receiver

1. The administrative receiver is deemed to be the agent of the company unless and until the company goes into liquidation. (IA s 44(1))

2. So far as most existing and continuing contracts of the company are concerned (*eg.* leases, hire purchase agreements, etc) the receiver will not incur personal liability unless he takes the positive step of adopting the contract. This, of course, he will never do.

3. *Liability on contracts* . The administrative receiver is, however, liable on any contract made by him in the carrying out of his functions except in so far as the contract otherwise provides. Thus, if the administrative receiver orders goods or services on behalf of the company in receivership he is personally at risk though he is entitled to be indemnified from the assets of the company. (IA s 44(1))

4. In practice an administrative receiver will clearly not wish to run the risk of being held personally liable upon contracts which he makes. Accordingly he will always seek to avoid personal liability by taking three specific steps:

    (a) immediately upon appointment, he writes to all senior employees stating that in future any order for goods or services must actually be signed by him

    (b) also immediately upon appointment he writes to all known suppliers of goods or services to the company stating that the company is in receivership and that in future he personally must sign any order for goods or services

    (c) when putting in an order for goods or services, the receiver will always add a disclaimer stating that he accepts no personal liability upon the contract.

5. *Contracts of employment.* A particular problem faced by an administrative receiver arises in connection with contracts of employment.

Section 44 of the Insolvency Act states that he is liable on any contract of employment adopted by him in carrying out his functions but that he is not to be taken to have adopted a contract of employment by reason of anything done or omitted to be done within 14 days after his employment.

6. Traditionally, administrative receivers would write to all employees immediately upon appointment stating that they were not adopting any contract of employment and that the employees remained the employees of the company.

7. However, in *Re Paramount Airways Limited, Powdrill* v *Watson* [1995] 2 All ER 65 the House of Lords held that an administrator (who in this regard is under a similar liability to an administrative receiver) could not disclaim liability upon contracts of employment and that he was taken to have adopted a contract of employment if he allowed it to run for more than 14 days after his employment.

8. *Insolvency Act 1994.* Such a ruling obviously caused enormous problems to the insolvency profession. Administrators and administrative receivers were taken to have adopted any contract of employment merely by not dismissing the employees by 14 days following their appointment. Accordingly, the Insolvency Act 1994 was hurriedly passed.

9. This provides in essence that an administrator or an administrative receiver who allows contracts of employment to continue more than 14 days following his appointment is only liable for matters such as wages and pension contributions relating to the period of time after adoption. In other words, he is not to be regarded as liable for accrued employment rights such as the employees' entitlement to redundancy pay.

10. *Defects of Act.* However, the Act is usually perceived as having two major defects:

   ● it only relates to contracts of employment adopted by administrators and administrative receivers. Accordingly, it has no impact upon contracts of employment adopted by a receiver and manager. A receiver and manager who adopts a contract of employment is fully liable upon that contract.

● the legislation is not retrospective. Accordingly a number of actions are now in progress against administrators and administrative receivers where executives claimed to have been wrongfully dismissed by the office helder. Ironically, in many cases such actions are brought by the very people whose mis-management led to the collapse of the company.

Duties of the administrative receiver

1. The statutory duties of the administrative receiver in relation to obtaining a copy of the statement of affairs, producing a report and calling a meeting of creditors have already been considered.

2. *Duty of care.* Basically any duty of care owed by an administrative receiver is owed to the appointing debenture holder and any creditor perporting to rank in priority. Thus, if an administrative receiver were to vacate office without having paid the preferential creditors, who of course rank ahead of the holder of a floating charge, while making a payment to the floating charge holder, the administrative receiver would himself be personally liable to the potential creditors. However, it is fair to say that there is almost no duty of care owed down the line to the unsecured creditors.

3. The rationale for this is that since an administrative receiver must vacate office as soon as he has paid the secured creditor by whom he was appointed, it is difficult to see how he can owe any significant duty of care to the unsecured creditors.

4. *Vacation of office.* The administrative receiver must vacate office on the completion of the administrative receivership.

5. Upon vacating office, he must give notice to:

   (a) the company

   (b) if the company is in liquidation, the liquidator

   (c) any members of the creditors' committee

   (d) the Registrar of Companies. (IA s 45(4) and IR 3.35)

Liquidations

1. Liquidation is an area of law which a non–specialist often finds confusing.

2. This is probably largely because there are two types of liquidation, voluntary and compulsory, and the voluntary liquidation is itself divided into members' voluntary liquidation and creditors' voluntary liquidation.

3. *Procedure.* In considering liquidations it is advisable to bear in mind that every liquidation goes through three stages:

    (a) the liquidator is appointed

    (b) he does what he can to maximise the assets of the company

    (c) he distributes the assets in the order laid down by the law and has the company struck off the register.

4. The steps open to the liquidator to maximise the assets and the order of distribution are the same in all three types of liquidation. What distinguishes them is the method in which the liquidator is appointed.

5. With a members' voluntary liquidation, the company is solvent. Accordingly, it has little place in any consideration of insolvent liquidation.

6. *Insolvent liquidations.* Of all the insolvent liquidations, about two-thirds are at any one time creditors' voluntary liquidations and one-

third compulsory. The factor which distinguishes the creditors' voluntary liquidation from the compulsory liquidation is that in the case of the former the court is not directly involved. The liquidator can go to the court to set aside matters such as transactions in an under value or preferences but the court is not directly involved unless so invited. On the other hand, with the compulsory winding up the court is directly involved and an investigation is carried out by the Official Receiver into the directors' dealings in the period leading up to the commencement of the liquidation.

7.   In a given situation of corporate insolvency, what sort of liquidation takes place, whether creditors' voluntary or compulsory, depends largely upon chance or perhaps, more accurately, the personalities involved. If the directors are properly advised that the company must go into liquidation and they take that advice, then the distinct likelihood is that a creditors' voluntary liquidation will follow. On the other hand, if the directors are not properly advised, or if they fail to take the advice given, and if there is some creditor who has the resources and the will to petition, it is likely that a compulsory liquidation will follow.

8.   It must be emphasised that, in general terms, the directors of a company which is going to go into liquidation are best advised to avoid a compulsory liquidation if at all possible because of its investigative nature.

Commencement of a members' voluntary liquidation

1.   As has been said, this sort of liquidation occurs only when the company is solvent. Accordingly, it could perhaps be argued that a consideration of it is out of place in a book on corporate insolvency. However, for the sake of completeness it will be referred to briefly.

2.   *Declaration of solvency.* Before a members' voluntary liquidation can be commenced, the directors of the company must make a declaration of solvency. This is a statement that all the debts of the company will be paid in full within 12 months of the passing of the resolution of the members to commence the winding up or such

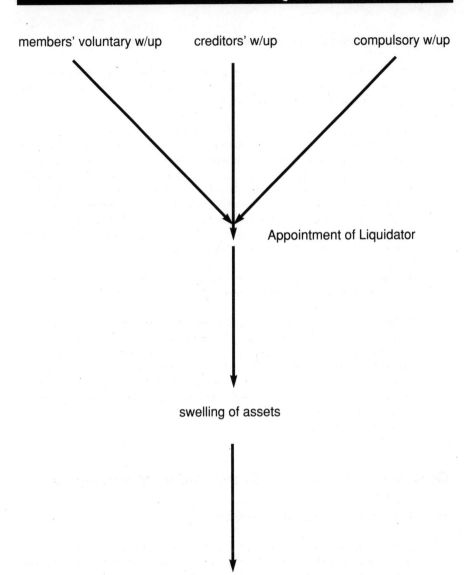

members' voluntary w/up   creditors' w/up   compulsory w/up

Appointment of Liquidator

swelling of assets

distribution and dissolution of company

shorter period as they may choose to state. (IA s 89)

3.   This declaration must be submitted to the Registrar of Companies within 15 days following the date on which the resolution of winding up was passed. (IA s 89(3))

4.   *Special resolution.* A members' voluntary winding up is almost always commenced by the passing of a special resolution by the members. Very occasionally, however, it may be commenced by the passing of an ordinary resolution. This occurs in two situations only, first where the company was for a fixed duration and secondly where the company was formed in anticipation of a specified occurrence. In these cases, an ordinary resolution is sufficient if the company has lasted for the anticipated duration or the anticipated occurrence has taken place as the case may be. (IA s 84(1))

5.   At the meeting when the resolution to wind up is passed, the members also pass an ordinary resolution to appoint the liquidator.

6.   By section 95 if at any time the liquidator forms the opinion that the company will be unable to pay its debts within the period stated by the directors in their declaration of insolvency, he must call a creditors meeting to be held within 28 days. As from the date of this meeting, the liquidation continues as though it were a creditors' voluntary liquidation. A consequence of this is that the creditors will be able to nominate a liquidator in place of the existing one and appoint a committee.

Commencement of a creditors' voluntary winding up

1.   Here there is no declaration of solvency.

2.   *Extraordianry resolution.* The members resolve by extraordinary resolution that the company should be wound up because it cannot, by reason of its liabilities, continue its business.

3.   At the same meeting an ordinary resolution is passed to appoint a liquidator.

4. *Creditors' meeting.* Within 14 days, a meeting of the creditors must be held. The creditors must be given at least seven days' notice by post of this meeting. (IA s 98)

5. The meeting must also be advertised in the *Gazette* and once at least in two newspapers circulating in the locality in which the company's principal place of business was situated. (IA s 85(1))

6. Where the company is put into creditors' voluntary liquidation, it is theoretically possible that the members' nominee may be the liquidator elect for a period of up to 14 days. The majority of powers conferred on the liquidator may be exercised during this period prior to the creditors' meeting only with the consent of the court. (IA s 166)

7. *Information to creditors.* If the company is to be put into creditors' voluntary liquidation, the notice summoning the creditors' meeting must state either the name and address of a person qualified to act as an insolvency practitioner in relation to the company who, during the period before the meeting, will give the creditors any information which they may reasonably require concerning the affairs of the company or alternatively a place in the locality where the company's principal place of business was situated, or a list of the names and addresses of the company's creditors will be able to be inspected. (IA s 98(2))

8. The directors must prepare and lay before the creditors' meeting a statement of affairs verified by affidavit. (IA s 99)

9. *Choice of liquidator.* At the creditors' meeting, the majority in value voting may appoint a liquidator. A liquidation committee of not more than five creditors may also be appointed at this meeting. Where such a committee is appointed, the members of the company may themselves appoint up to five persons to act as members to serve on the committee. However, the creditors may resolve that all or any of the persons appointed by the company should not be members of the liquidation committee.(IA s 101)

10. It is obviously possible that the creditors, at their meeting, may appoint a different person to be liquidator from the one proposed by the members. In such a case the members' nominee must stand down and it is the creditors' liquidator who takes up post. (IA s 100)

(a) Members' Voluntary Winding up

Directors' declaration of solvency

↕ 5 weeks maximum

Members' meeting
(i) Special resolution to wind up
(ii) Ordinary resolution to appoint liquidator

(b) Creditors' Voluntary Winding Up

N.B. No declaration of solvency

Members' meeting
(i) Extraordinary resolution to wind up
(ii) Ordinary resolution to appoint liquidator

↕ 14 days maximum

Creditors' meeting
(i) Simple majority to appoint liquidator
(ii) Simple majority to appoint liquidation committee

A rule common to both members' and creditors' liquidations

If a company is in voluntary liquidation and no liquidator has been appointed, the directors may not exercise any of their powers except as they may be allowed by the court, or in the case of a creditors' voluntary liquidation, in so far as may be necessary to call a creditors' meeting. They may, however, dispose of perishable goods and do anything necessary to protect the company's assets. (IA s 114)

Commencement of a compulsory winding up

1. Section 122 of the Insolvency Act contains a number of grounds for the winding up of a company. In the context of insolvency the only one of any relevance is that the company is unable to pay its debts.

2. The petitioner must be a creditor who is owed at least £750. (IA s 123(1) and *Re Milford Docks Co* (1883) 23 CR D 292)

3. The inability of a company to pay its debts is shown in one of four ways:

   Showing insolvency. (a) where a statutory demand requiring the company to pay a sum in excess of £750 has been served upon the company and the company has not made the required payment or offered security for it within three weeks

   (b) where execution on a judgment in favour of a creditor of a company is returned unsatisfied

   (c) where it is proved to the satisfaction of the court that the company is unable to pay its debts as they fall due

   (d) where the value of the company's assets is less than the value of its liabilities, taking into account its contingent and prospective liabilities. (IA s 123)

4. In regard to the first of these grounds, inability to satisfy a statutory demand, it should be noted that it is not the statutory demand which

is the basis of the winding up petition but the failure to satisfy the statutory demand within three weeks.

5. *Use of statutory demand.* Obviously a statutory demand can be used by a company which is in difficulties almost as a means of obtaining credit. In the case of companies (unlike a creditor's petition to make an individual bankrupt) there is no way in which the three week period can be truncated. There is therefore a risk that during the three week period before a petition can be presented assets may be disposed of by the company to the detriment to the generality of its creditors.

6. For this reason, the third ground referred to above, namely where it is proved to the satisfaction of the court that the company is unable to pay its debts as they fall due, may prove useful. A petitioning creditor may prove the insolvency of the company on this ground for example by satisfying the court that the company always waits for a statutory demand before paying a particular creditor or that it is obvious that the directors each month shuffle the invoices of the company to see which creditors will be paid that month: (see *eg. Re Taylor's Industrial Flooring Ltd* [1990] BCC 44)

7. The final ground referred to above, namely that there is a balance sheet insolvency, is of very little relevance in practice. Since the petitioning creditor must be owed at least £750, so long as the company is paying its debts as they fall due, there will be no creditor able to petition on this ground even if the company is insolvent on its balance sheet.

8. *Official Receiver.* Following the making of a winding up order by the court, the Official Receiver becomes the liquidator of the company. (IA s 136)

9. The Official Receiver may then require any persons who are or have been officers of the company or who have been employed by the company to produce a statement of affairs. This must be verified by affidavit by the persons who are required to submit it and must give particulars of:

    (a) the company's assets, debts and liabilities

    (b) the company's creditors, including their names and addresses

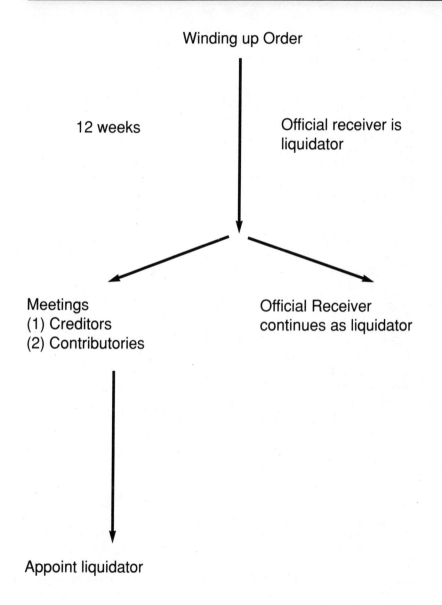

Winding up Order

12 weeks

Official receiver is liquidator

Meetings
(1) Creditors
(2) Contributories

Official Receiver continues as liquidator

Appoint liquidator

(c) any securities held by the creditors

(d) the dates when the securities were given. (IA s 131)

10. *Meetings.* Within 12 weeks of the making of the winding up order, the Official Receiver must decide whether he is going to summon meetings of creditors and contributories. If he decides not to, he must give notice of this both to the court and to the creditors and contributories. (IA s 136)

11. The purpose of this procedure is to determine who is going to be the liquidator, whether the Official Receiver will perform this task himself or whether an insolvency practitioner will be appointed.

12. *Practical considerations.* There are detailed provisions in the Insolvency Act dealing with such matters as rights of the creditors to insist upon a meeting if the Official Receiver decides not to call one and the appointment of an insolvency practitioner to be the liquidator if the meetings of the creditors and contributories cannot agree on who should be appointed (see IA s 139). However in practice these are not of great consequence. In practical terms what is of consequence is what decides the Official Receiver to complete the winding up himself or to farm it out to an insolvency practitioner. The answer to this is the value of the assets of the company. Bearing in mind that the costs of the winding up are the first thing to be paid from the assets of the company realised by the liquidator and also that with a large company which is in liquidation there are always some assets irrespective of the amount of the liabilities, the Official Receiver will usually only wish to handle the job himself if there are insufficient assets to pay for an insolvency practitioner.

13. As has been said, the essential difference between a compulsory and a voluntary winding up is the investigative nature of the former. The main purpose of the statement of affairs is to assist the Official Receiver in his duty of investigation into the promotion, formation and business dealings of the company and, where the company has failed, the causes of its failure. The Official Receiver must make such report as he thinks fit to the court of the results of these investigations. (IA s 132)

14.   The liquidator may apply to the court for the public examination of any person who is or has been an officer of the company, or been liquidator of the company, or been involved in the management of the company. (IA s 133)

Maximising the assets of the company for the benefit of the creditors

1.   Regardless of how the liquidator has been appointed and what type of liquidation is proceeding, the task of the liquidator is to maximise the assets of the company for the benefit of the creditors.

2.   To achieve this there are a number of procedures open to him which will now be considered including seeking to have set aside transactions at an under value or preferences, disclaiming unprofitable contracts and onerous assets and taking proceedings against directors and others for fraudulent and wrongful trading and misfeasance.

3.   It will be appreciated that in respect of any procedure the liquidator is likely to be acting from a position of weakness. The more insolvent the company, the less funds the liquidator is likely to have at his disposal to proceed against the directors. For this reason liquidators are often criticised for seemingly not seeking to recover assets in circumstances where they have simply taken a value judgement not to proceed because in their view the risk of taking action out-weighs any potential benefit to the company and its creditors.

4.   *Application to court.* The appropriate action for any creditor or member who is unhappy with some act or omission of a liquidator is to apply to the court under Insolvency Act sections 112 and 168(5). An application can be made to the court to determine any question arising in the winding up of a company, and, upon such application, the court may make such order as it thinks fit.

Commencement of the winding up

1.   A liquidator can seek to upset certain transactions entered into by the company within various periods of time prior to the commencement of the winding up.

2.   *Commencement.* A crucial date therefore is that when the winding up commenced. It is:

(a)   in the case of a voluntary winding up, the date of the passing of the resolution (IA s 86), and

(b)   in the case of a compulsory winding up, the date of the presentation of the petition (IA s 129).

Transactions at an undervalue (IA s 238)

1.   These occur where, within the two years prior to the commencement of the winding up, the company has entered into a transaction which was:

● either a gift by the company
● or under which the company received a consideration whose value was less than the consideration given by the company. (IA s 238(4))

2.   The transaction may only be upset if at the time or as a result of the transaction the company was unable to pay its debts as they fell due. (IA s 240(2))

3.   As a general rule, it is for the liquidator to prove this inability to pay debts.

4.   *Connected persons.* However, if the transaction was in favour of a person connected with the company, this insolvency is presumed. (IA s 240(2)))

5.   Connected persons are directors and shadow directors of the company and their associates. (IA s 249). An associate includes that person's spouse, his business partner or spouse of his business partner, a company in his control and a trustee for any of these. (IA s 435)

6. *Belief company would benefit.* A transaction cannot be upset under this heading if it was entered into by the company in good faith for the purpose of carrying on its business and at the time of the transaction there were reasonable grounds to believe in that it would benefit the company. (IA s 238(5))

7. There is no need to prove intent to defraud creditors nor is there a need to prove knowledge by the directors of the insolvency.

8. On an application by the liquidator in respect of a transaction and under value the court may make such order as it thinks fit for restoring the position for what it would have been if the company had not entered into that transaction. (IA s 238(3))

Preferences (IA s 239)

1. A preference arises where a company does anything or suffers anything to be done which has the effect of putting a creditor in a better position than he would otherwise have occupied in the event of the company's going into insolvent liquidation. (IA s 239(4))

2. *State of mind.* The state of mind of the directors is crucial. They must have been influenced by a desire to put the creditor in such better position. The meaning of "influenced by a desire" was considered in *Re MC Bacon Limited* [1990] BCC 78. Two particular observations need to be made in respect of the state of mind:

(a) the intention to prefer the creditor concerned need not wholly consume the mind of the company. In other words it can be merely part of the intention,

(b) however, there must be a desire to put the creditor concerned in a better position. Desire is subjective. The state of mind of the company must be examined. Desire needs to be distinguished from intention which is objective. A person may intend the consequences of his actions without necessarily desiring them. For example, he may choose the lesser of two evils without desiring either.

3. Generally it is for the liquidator to prove to the court that the directors were influenced by the appropriate desire. However, in the case of a preference to a person connected with the company, such a desire is presumed. (IA s 239(6))

4.   The period during which the transaction must have been entered into is generally six months prior to the commencement of the winding up. However, if the preference was in favour of a connected person, this period is extended to two years prior to the commencement of the winding up. (IA s 240(1))

5.   Once again, it must generally be shown by the liquidator that the company was insolvent at the time of the transaction or became insolvent as a result of it. This is presumed where the transaction was in favour of a connected person. (IA s 240(2))

6.   *Directors' guarantees.* Amongst the persons who may be preferred may be a guarantor of the company's indebtedness. For example, in *Re M Kushler Limited* [1943] Ch 248 a director had given a personal guarantee of his company's overdraft. When he became aware that the company would be unable to avoid a liquidation, he paid cheques received in the ordinary course of business into the company's bank account but without drawing against them as would normally occur. After some days the overdraft was cleared and the director then cancelled his guarantee and arranged for the company to go into creditors' voluntary liquidation. It was held that there had been a preference of the director concerned. Had he have arranged for the company to go into creditors' voluntary liquidation as soon as he became aware that it was necessary, he would have become liable upon the guarantee which he had given to the company's bank. As such he would have then been subrogated to the position of the bank and able to claim as a creditor in the liquidation. His avoidance of this liability was a preference and it was held that he should contribute in the liquidation a sum equal to what the overdraft stood at when he became aware that a liquidation was inevitable.

7.   Having said this, since it is the state of mind of the directors which is crucial, there will not be a preference if, for example, in similar circumstances it is the bank manager who, aware of the company's difficulties, forces down the overdraft facility available to the company.

8.   The fact that something has been done by way of a court order does not, without more, prevent the doing of that thing from constituting the giving of a preference. (IA s 239(7)) In other words, an insolvency court could set aside as a preference a charging order

made over the property of the company by another court in earlier proceedings.

Remedies in the case of transactions at an under value and preferences (IA s 241)

In particular the court may:

1. require a return of money or property to the company;

2. require a transfer to the company of property representing the subject matter of the transaction;

3. discharge any security given by the company;

4. require a payment to be made to the liquidator in respect of benefits received;

5. impose new or revived obligations on any guarantor;

6. require security to be provided;

7. provide that any person who falls under an obligation as a result of any of these orders may prove in the winding up as an unsecured creditor;

    Order may affect third parties. Such an order may affect the property of, or impose any obligation on, any person whether or not he is the person which whom the company in question entered into the transaction or the person to whom the preference was given. However, the order may not prejudice the interest in property which was acquired from a person other than the company and was acquired in good faith and for value. (IA s 241(2))

It used to be the case that this provision only afforded protection to persons taking not only in good faith and for value but also without notice of the relevant circumstances giving rise to the transaction at an under value or the preference. However, the Insolvency (No. 2) Act 1994 removed the need for the person seeking protection not to have notice of the circumstances giving rise to the unlawful transaction. This protection is not, however, afforded where the third party is connected with or was an associate of the company or such connected person. (See IA s 241(2A))

Transactions to avoid the payment of debts (IA s 423)

1. The court may set aside any transaction entered into by the company with the intention of defeating the rightful claims of creditors.

2. *Petitioners.* This provision is a revised version of section 172 of the Law of Property Act 1925 which provided for the setting aside of fraudulent conveyances. Accordingly it is not limited to situations where the company is in liquidation and, unlike most other procedures to recover assets on an insolvency such as transactions at an under value and preferences, it does not have to be instituted by the liquidator. While a liquidator can instigate proceedings, so to can any person who is a victim of the transaction. If the company is in liquidation, an application should generally be made by the liquidator, but a victim of the transaction may make an application with the consent of the court. (IA s 424)

3. *No time limit.* There is no time limit concerning when the transaction should have been entered into. Thus, at least technically, it is possible that the court could set aside a transaction entered into several years before the onset of insolvency.

4. It is not necessary to show that the company was insolvent at the time of the transaction. However, it is necessary to show that the transaction was at an under value. (IA s 423(1))

5. *Court orders.* If proceedings are successfully brought under this provision, the court may make such order as it thinks fit to restore the position to what it would have been if the transaction had not been entered into and to protect the interests of persons who are victims of the transaction.

There are detailed specific orders which the court may make, very similar to those described above which may be made in the case of a transaction of an under value or a preference. (IA s 425(1))

6.   No order made under section 423 may prejudice any interest in property acquired from a person other than the company which was acquired in good faith, and for value and without notice of the relevant circumstances giving rise to the transaction to defeat the claims of creditors. (IA s 425(2)). It should be noted that the Insolvency (No 2) Act 1994 has no application in respect of this remedy and so a respondent seeking protection must not only show that he took in good faith and for value but also that he took without notice of the relevant circumstances.

7.   *State of mind.* The essence of a transaction to avoid the payment of debts is the state of mind of the directors of the company at the time of making the transaction. Before making an order, the court must be satisfied that the company entered into the transaction:

(a) either for the purpose of putting its assets beyond the reach of present and prospective creditors

(b) or for the purpose of prejudicing the interests of such a person. (IA s 423(3))

Extortionate credit transactions (IA s 244)

1.   A liquidator can seek to upset extortionate credit transactions entered into during the three years prior to the company going into liquidation.   (In regard to the three year time limit, it should be noted that the statutory provision refers to the three years leading up to the company going into liquidation rather than to the three years leading up to the commencement of the liquidation. (IA s 244(2))

2.   A credit transaction is extortionate if, having regard to the risk accepted by the person providing the credit:

(a) its terms were grossly exorbitant; or

(b) it otherwise grossly contravened the ordinary principles of fair dealing. (IA s 244(3))

3.   *Court orders.* When the court proclaims a credit transaction to be extortionate it may make any of the following orders:

(a)   set aside the whole or any part of the obligation created by the transaction

(b)   vary the terms of the transaction

(c)   require the other party to the transaction to pay to the liquidator sums paid to it by the company

(d)   require the other party to the transaction to surrender any security held by him

(e)   direct that accounts should be taken. (IA s 244(4))

Invalidation of floating charges (IA s 245)

1.   A floating charge is *prima facie* invalid if created within 12 months prior to the commencement of a winding up. (IA s 245(3))

2.   This is not, however the case, if either:

(a) the company was solvent at the time of the creation of the charge; or

(b) the company received benefit at the same time as or after the creation of the charge. (IA s 245(2))

3.   The period is extended to two years prior to the commencement of the winding up where the charge was created in favour of a person connected with the company. (IA s 245(3))

4.   *Effect of Clayton's case.* Often the floating charge is created to secure bank lending. In this regard, the rule in *Clayton's case* must be remembered. (See *Devaynes* v *Noble, Clayton's case*) (1816) 1 Mer 529. This rule is that, in the absence of contrary intention, a bank account is operated strictly chronologically. The result of this is that the normal operation of an account can soon render valid a potentially void floating charge under this provision. For example in *Re Yeovil Glove Co Limited* [1965] Ch 148 a floating charge was created to secure an existing bank overdraft. The company then operated the account for several months, paying into the account sums in excess of the amount of the overdraft at the time of the

creation of the charge. Similar amounts were drawn out of the account during this time and within 12 months of the creation of the charge the company went into liquidation. The question arose as to whether the charge was good to secure the overdraft as it stood at the commencement of the liquidation. It was held that, applying the rule in *Clayton's case,* so soon as sufficient funds had been paid into the account equal to the amount of the overdraft at the time of the creation of the charge, the pre-existing overdraft had been cleared. Accordingly any future drawings from the account were made after the creation of the charge and thus the charge was valid to cover the amount of the overdraft at the time of the commencement of the liquidation.

Disclaimer (IA s 178)

1. A liquidator can disclaim onerous property notwithstanding that he has:

   - taken possession of it
   - endeavoured to sell it
   - exercised in any other way any rights over it. (IA s 178(2))

2. *Disclaimer property.* Amongst the property which can be disclaimed is:

   - any unprofitable contract
   - any other unsaleable property
   - any property which is not readily saleable.(IA s 178(3))

3. *Procedure.* Before 1986, it used to be the case that disclaimer could only take place with the consent of the court. This has, however, been changed. Basically disclaimer is effected by a liquidator completing the appropriate form 4.53, submitting this to the court and then serving a copy on the person against whom disclaimer is sought.

4. A third party to any transaction involving the company may ask a liquidator whether he intends to disclaim. In such a situation the liquidator must then reach a decision within 28 days otherwise he

loses the right to disclaim. (IA s 178(5))

5. Any person who suffers loss in consequence of a disclaimer is regarded as a creditor of the company to the extent of that loss and thus may prove for the loss in the winding up. (IA s 178(6))

Misfeasance proceedings (IA s 212)

1. If, while a company is solvent, any director or other person involved with the company misapplies property of the company or goes in breach of any fiduciary or any other duty, the proper plaintiff to take proceedings aginst him is the company or, alternatively, a shareholder taking advantage of a minority protection procedure such as unfair prejudice under the Companies Act section 459.

2. The equivalent of such a procedure when a company is being wound up is misfeasance proceedings under section 212.

3. The provision applies when any person who has been an officer, liquidator, administrator, or administrative receiver of a company or has been concerned in its promotion, formation or management has misapplied or retained any money or other property of the company or been guilty of any misfeasance or breach of any fiduciary or other duty in relation to the company. (IA s 212(1))

4. *Petitioner.* Proceedings under this section may be commenced by the Official Receiver or the liquidator of the company or any creditor or contributory of the company. (IA s 212(3))

Remedies. When liability is found under this provision, the court may require the respondent to repay money or restore property to the company together with interest at such rate as the court thinks just or to contribute such sum to the assets of the company by way of compensation as is thought just. (IA s 212(3))

Directors and Insolvency

Introduction

1. There are four significant risks which are faced by directors when their company becomes insolvency.

2. These are:

    - liability upon personal guarantees

    - liability for fraudulent trading

    - liability for wrongful trading

    - risk of disqualification.

3. Civil liability for fraudulent and wrongful trading can only arise if the company is in liquidation.

4. However, liability on personal guarantees and the risk of disqualification can generally arise whatever form the insolvency takes.

Personal guarantees

1. It often happens in the case of small private companies that the directors will have given a personal guarantee of the company's overdraft borrowing.

2. In the event of the company becoming insolvent it is probable that these guarantees will be enforced against the directors.

Fraudulent trading

1. Fraudulent trading gives rise to both a civil and a criminal liability. Under the Insolvency Act 1986 section 213 a liquidator can seek a civil award against a director who is responsible for fraudulent trading. Under the Companies Act 1985 section 458 a criminal offence is committed by a director found guilty of fraudulent trading.

2. Both sections refer to fraudulent trading as occurring where any business of the company has been carried on with intent to defraud creditors.

3. *State of mind.* The precise meaning of carrying on the business with intent to defraud creditors has been the subject of definition by the courts. In *Re WC Leitch Brothers Ltd* [1932] 2 Ch 71 it was said to occur where a company carries on business and incurs debts at a time when, to the knowledge of the directors, there was no reasonable prospect of the debts being paid as and when they fell due for payment. Alternatively it was said that it could occur where directors were reckless as to whether the debts could be paid. In other words where the directors, in ordering goods or services, showed a wilful disregard as to whether the company would be able to pay for them in due course. In *Re Patrick & Lyon Limited* [1933] Ch 786 the court said that fraudulent trading involved actual dishonesty such as commercial men would regard as imputing real moral blame.

4. Thus it is the state of mind of the directors which has to be established for liability to be imposed upon them for fraudulent trading.

5. *Standard of proof.* Since fraudulent trading gives rise to both a civil and a criminal liability, and is expressed in identical terms in both sections, the standard of proof required to be shown by the liquidator is the criminal standard *ie.* beyond reasonable doubt,

rather than the civil standard, balance of probabilities.

6.   Accordingly, fraudulent trading is exceedingly difficult to establish. For this reason there was introduced in 1986 the alternative civil liability for wrongful trading.

Wrongful trading

1.   Wrongful trading is only a civil liability. There is no criminal offence. It is designed therefore to catch directors who have been careless rather than dishonest.

2.   By the Insolvency Act section 214, three things must be established by the liquidator who wishes to show that a director is liable for wrongful trading:

(a) that the respondent was a director of the company

(b) that the company is now in insolvent liquidation

(c) that the director concerned knew or should have known that there was no reasonable prospect of the company avoiding going into insolvent liquidation.

3.   These three matters will now be considered in more detail.

That the respondent was a director of the company

1.   By section 251 a director includes any person occupying the position of a director, by whatever name he is called.

2.   Thus, amongst the people who are potentially liable for wrongful trading will be a person such as a majority shareholder who de facto controls the business of the company though he has never been formally appointed as a director and his name does not appear in the register of directors.

3.   *Shadow directors.* By section 214(7) a director includes, in this context, a shadow director. By section 251 a shadow director is defined as a person in accordance with whose directions or instructions the directors of the company are accustomed to act. This seemingly reinforces the comment made in the above note

where it was suggested that a dominating shareholder could be regarded as a director. However, it is possible that the definition of the shadow director could embrace other persons such as:

● a bank which too closely monitors a floating charge which it has over the undertaking of a customer company by telling the directors what they should be doing

●a parent company which in effect controls the board of its subsidiary

●a company doctor called in to try to help the directors of a company in difficulties to find some way out of its problems.

Professional advisers. However, there is an express proviso that a person does not become a shadow director merely because the directors act on advice given by him in a professional capacity. Thus, an auditor or the company solicitor is probably not at serious risk of being found liable for wrongful trading.

That the company is insolvent liquidation

1. In this context, an insolvent liquidation is said by section 214(6) to occur when the assets of the company are insufficient to meet its debts and liabilities and also the expenses of the winding up.

2. On reflection it will be appreciated that this is an horrendous definition of insolvency. The reference to the assets refers to the realised value of the assets rather than their book value. For the company to be solvent these must be sufficient to meet not only its current liabilities but also its contingent liabilities including liabilities which arise on the winding up, such as claims by staff for redundancy payments or payments for wrongful dismissal and claims for damages by landlords in respect of disclaimed leases. Moreover the assets as realised must, as well as meeting these liabilities, cover all the expenses of the winding up.

That the director knew that this was going to happen

1. When we say that a person should have realised that something was going to happen, we have to consider the standard of skill expected of the director.

2. Traditionally the standard of skill expected of directors has been low in English law. For example in the leading case of *Re City Equitable Fire Insurance* [1925] Ch 407 it was said that a director had simply to show the skill which may reasonably be expected of a person of his knowledge and experience.

3. Thus, if a director is sued by his company for breach of his duty, skill and care (what would more likely today be referred to as negligence) he might well avoid liability simply by showing that he was inexperienced/dim/stupid.

4. However, the possibility of a company actually taking proceedings against one of its directors is fairly remote.

5. However, this is not the case where the company is in liquidation and proceedings are initiated by the liquidator.

6. *Standard of skill.* Here the standard of care which has to be shown by the director wishing to avoid liability is the higher of:

    ● the general knowledge, skill and experience possessed by the director himself; or

    ● the general knowledge, skill and experience that may reasonably be expected of the person carrying out the same functions as are carried out by that director in relation to that company. (IA s 214(4))

7. It will be appreciated that the first of these tests is subjective and the second objective. In the case of the first test, the director must show the level of skill which he actually possesses. Thus if, for example, the director is a qualified accountant, he has to show the sort of skill which would be expected of such a qualified person. The second test is objective and it is this which will usually be the test to be applied. The director must show the sort of skill which a sensible onlooker would expect a director in his position to be exercising. This is not to say that a director of a small engineering company has to show the same skill as a main board director of a major PLC. However, it does presume that a director will show at least a modicum of ability.

A defence to wrongful trading?

1. There is a defence of sorts provided by section 214(3) that as soon as a director realised that there was no reasonable prospect that the company would avoid going into insolvent liquidation he took every step with a view to minimising the potential loss to the company's creditors that he ought to have taken.

2. In practice the defence is virtually impossible to prove. Had the wording used referred to the director taking all reasonable steps then on occasions the defence might be usable. However, he has to show that he took *every* step. Thus the director, who to the point where he realised that an insolvent liquidation was inevitable had probably not demonstrated any great skill in his running of the company, must at this point show almost superhuman intellectual ability if he is to avoid liability. Moreover, it was said in *Re Produce Marketing Consortium Limited* [1989] 1 WLR 745 that a director against whom wrongful trading procedures are taken cannot take advantage of the general defence provided by the Companies Act section 727 that he acted honestly and reasonably and ought fairly to be excused.

The degree of liability

1. The liability of the directors seems to be arrived at by the court dropping a plumb-line as at that point when the directors should have realised that the situation was irrecoverable. Any further deficit incurred after that point will be the liability of the directors. This was the finding of the court in *Re Produce Marketing Consortium (Nº2)* [1989] BCLC 520 and *Re DKG Contractors Limited* [1990] BCC 903.

2. Clearly different directors may incur a greater or lesser degree of liability, though it is clearly no defence for a director simply to show that he was unaware of the problems faced by the company.

3. Moreover in *Re DKG Contractors Limited* it was said that it is no defence for a director simply to show that he resigned prior to the liquidation nor that he had no perception of what being a director involved.

Disqualification of directors

1. Another problem faced by directors is disqualification under the Company Directors Disqualification Act 1986.

2. *Effect of disqualification.* The effect of disqualification is that any person who takes part in the management of the company while disqualified commits a criminal offence and can be made personally liable for any debts of the company in respect of which he acts. (CDAA ss 13 and 15)

3. Disqualification does not prevent him from earning a living. He can continue to trade as a sole trader or in partnership unless professional rules prohibit this as, for example, is the case with solicitors.

4. *Traditional grounds.* For a long time there have been various grounds for disqualification including:

    (a) on conviction of an indictable offence in connection with the promotion, formation, management or liquidation of the company (maximum 15 years) (CDAA s 2)

    (b) persistent breaches of companies legislation (maximum five years) (CDAA s 3)

    (c) on a conviction for fraudulent trading or any fraudulent connection with the company (maximum 15 years) (CDAA s 4)

    (d) on persistent convictions for failing to make returns to the Registrar of Companies (maximum 5 years) (CDAA s 5)

    (e) on being found liable in the civil courts for wrongful or fraudulent trading (maximum 15 years) (CDAA s 10)

    (f) it is also an offence for an undischarged bankrupt to participate in the management of the company unless he does so with the consent of the court. (CDAA s 11)

5. There is also a major new ground for disqualification where a director is found to be unfit to be a director of a company following either an investigation by the Department of Trade and Industry or the insolvency of the Company. (CDAA ss 6 and 8)

6. In the latter case the procedure is that every liquidator, administrative receiver and administrator must submit a report to the Secretary of State in respect of a person who is or has been a director of a company with which he has been dealing and who appears to be unfit to be a director.

7. *Reprehensible conduct.* The sort of conduct which the office-holder is to draw to attention of the Secretary of State includes:

- misfeasance or breach of fiduciary or other duty

- misapplication of company property

- the responsibility of the director for the company entering into transactions which may be set aside

- the responsibility of the director for the failure of the company to keep and make returns of accounts and other records of the company

- the responsibility of the director for the insolvency of the company

- the responsibility of the director for any failure of the company to supply goods or services paid for in advance.

8. The Secretary of State will then take action in appropriate circumstances for the disqualification of the director concerned.

9. Here, there is a minimum period of disqualification of two years and a maximum of 15 years.

Restriction on the re-use of company names

1. By section 216 any person who has been involved as a director or shadow director of a company during the 12 months prior to its going into liquidation commits a criminal offence if within the next five years he is similarly involved with a company having the same name as that of the company which went into liquidation or a name so similar so as to suggest an association with that company.

2. However, it is possible for the consent of the court to be obtained by

a person wishing to form a company having such a name. When such application is made the Secretary of State or the Official Receiver may appear and call the attention of the court to any matters which seem to him to be relevant. (IA s 216(5))

3. As well as committing the criminal offence referred to above, a person so involved with a company becomes personally liable for those debts and other liabilities incurred at a time when he was involved in the management of the company. (IA s 217)

Order in which Debts are paid on an Insolvency

Basically the order of payment of debts is as follows:

1. The costs of the insolvency.

2. Fixed charges in the order of creation and registration.

3. The preferential debts. These include:

    ● £800 arrears of wages per employee (or four months wages if less)

    ● accrued holiday pay

    ● PAYE deducted from emoluments paid during the 12 months before the commencement of the winding up

    ● VAT due in the period of six months before the commencement of the winding up

    ● Social Security contributions due in respect of the 12 months before the commencement of the winding up. (see IA Sched 6)

    There is no order for the payment of these debts. If the assets of the company are insufficient to meet all of them then they abate rateably

4. Floating charges in the order of creation and registration.

5.   Unsecured debts. These include:

- trade creditors
- any other taxes including assessed taxes
- taxes accruing for period outside the preferential periods referred to above

Again in the event of there being insufficient assets to meet these debts they abate rateably.

- local rates and taxes.

6.   In the event of anything remaining after all these debts have been paid, these funds are returned to the members.

Dissolution

At the end of the liquidation, the liquidator applies to the Registrar of Companies for the dissolution of the company. The application is made either by the liquidator or the official receiver.

Index